21ST
CENTURY
DEBATES

D0183506

TOURISM

OUR IMPACT ON THE PLANET

ROB BOWDEN

WAYLAND

5790

21st Century Debates Series

Genetics • Surveillance • Internet • Media • Artificial Intelligence • Climate Change • Energy • Rainforests • Waste, Recycling and Reuse • Endangered Species • Air Pollution • An Overcrowded World? • Food Supply • Water Supply • World Health • Global Debt • Terrorism • New Religious Movements • The Drugs Trade • Racism • Violence in Society • Globalisation • Transportation

Produced for Hodder Wayland by White-Thomson Publishing Ltd, 2/3 St Andrew's Place, Lewes, East Sussex BN7 1UP

© 2003 White-Thomson Publishing Ltd

Published in Great Britain in 2003 by Hodder Wayland, an imprint of Hodder Children's Books.

This paperback edition published in 2007 by Wayland, an imprint of Hachette Children's Books

Project editor: Kelly Davis
Commissioning editor: Steve White-Thomson
Proofreader: David C. Sills, Proof Positive Reading Service
Series and book design: Chris Halls, Mind's Eye Design
Picture research: Shelley Noronha, Glass Onion Pictures
Bar charts: Nick Hawken

British Library Cataloguing in Publication Data
Bowden, Rob
   Tourism. - (21st century debates)
   1.Tourism - Juvenile literature
   I.Title
   338.4'7'91
ISBN 978 0 7502 5163 1

Printed in China

Hachette Children's Books, 338 Euston Road, London NW1 3BH

Picture acknowledgements: EASI-Images 5, 8, 11, 15, 31, 35, 42, 46, 59 (Rob Bowden); Thomas Cook 10; Corbis 34 (Lawrence Manning), 37 (David Samuel Robbins); James Davis Travel Photography 14; Eye Ubiquitous 18 (Laurence Fordyce), 25 and 51 (David Forman), 28 (Bruce Adams), 33 (Jonathan Prangnell), 55 (James Davis/Paul Seheult); HWPL 20 (Gordon Clements), 32 (Paul Kenward); Impact 19 (Mark Henley), 23 (Ray Roberts), 38 (J. Hitchings), 40 (Daniel White), 47 (Giles Moberly), 52 (Piers Cavendish), 53 (Peter Menzel), 57 (Charles Coates); Popperfoto 56; Still Pictures 4 (Reinhard Janke), 6 (Gerard and Margi Moss), 27 (Andy Crump), 30 (Martha Cooper), 58 (Nigel Dickinson); Topham 12, 48, 49; Travel Ink Photography 17 (Dean Miculinic), 43 and 45 (Andrew Brown); WTPix cover (both), 7, 9, 13, 16, 22, 36 (Chris Fairclough), 44 (Dana Smillie).

Cover: *foreground*, tourists crowd into St. Mark's Square in Venice, Italy; *background*, palm trees on a beach in Goa, India

CONTENTS

GLOBAL TOURISM

In Europe, most people's experience of tourism is going abroad on holiday – like these tourists checking in at Hamburg Airport, Germany.

'...tourism is one of the world's least regulated industries, which has serious implications for ecosystems, communities and cultures around the world.'

Lisa Mastny, WorldWatch Institute

Pack your bags!

Most people probably think of themselves as tourists when they are packing their bags for a foreign holiday. Such holidays have become a major feature of many wealthier societies, and many people feel that they deserve at least one trip abroad each year. It is this 'international tourism' that receives most attention from the media and the general public. Television programmes encourage people to travel to exotic new destinations, and travel agents' windows entice customers with special offers and last-minute bargains.

International tourism is the easiest form of tourism to measure, as it is relatively simple to record the number of people arriving in a country over a year. Using this measure, international tourism increased dramatically during the second half of the twentieth century, from 25 million arrivals in 1950 to 698 million in 2000.

A global industry

In 1999, tourism employed an estimated 8 per cent of the global workforce (around 200 million people) and accounted for around 10 per cent of world income, an amazing US$453 billion. It is also a very fast-growing industry, expanding by an average of 7 per cent per year between 1950 and 2000. And these extraordinary figures do not include another form of tourism – domestic tourism (or tourism within a country).

In many countries, the domestic tourist industry is now even bigger than the international tourist industry. In the UK, for example, there were 175 million domestic tourist trips in 2000, compared to just 25 million tourists from overseas. If day trips (trips that do not include an overnight stay) are added, then the total is bigger still. In the UK alone some 1.3 billion day trips are made every year!

Tourists now visit the most remote parts of the world, such as mountain tops, deserts, and rainforests. Tourism even spread into space in 2001 when an American millionaire become the first person to holiday high above the Earth in a Russian spacecraft.

VIEWPOINT

'Unfortunately, not everyone has access to travel, but for those who do, it fulfils a deep-seated ... need felt by our modern societies.'
Francesco Frangialli, Secretary-General of the World Tourism Organization

weblinks▸

For more facts and figures on international tourism go to www.waylinks.co.uk/series/21debates/tourism

Tourists sightseeing in the picturesque Cotswolds in the UK, a very popular destination for international and domestic tourists alike.

Leave only footprints

There is a saying among some travellers – 'take only memories and leave only footprints'. This

would be a good motto for tourists to follow, but unfortunately the growth of mass tourism has left much more than just footprints. Environments have been degraded or destroyed, local communities have been relocated or split up, and some traditional cultures have almost disappeared. As foreign visitors continue to flock to ever more remote locations, bringing their own demands and ways of life, these negative effects seem set to increase. To reduce such problems, urgent action needs to be taken to change the way the tourism industry currently works.

Unfortunately some tourists leave unwanted evidence of their stay. This polluted beach is in Rio de Janeiro, Brazil.

weblinks

For more information on the World Tourism Organization (WTO) go to www.waylinks.co.uk/series/21debates/tourism

VIEWPOINT

'Most tourism is currently "self-regulated" but it is evident from the poor quality of employment, disregard for local people … and severe … environmental impacts … that this is not always adequate.'
UK Department for International Development, 1999

Who is in charge?

One of the problems with the tourism industry is that it is difficult to regulate. However there is one organization that monitors the growth and spread of world tourism. The World Tourism Organization (WTO) consists of 139 national governments and 350 companies and organizations involved in travel and tourism. The WTO enables members to share ideas and develop new policies as well as providing information on the development of the industry worldwide. Their work will feature throughout this book.

National governments are increasingly taking a leading role in the development of tourism in their own countries (although their role is not always a positive one, as we will discover). There are also several non-governmental organizations that play an important part in promoting tourism for sustainable development. This is tourism that conserves environments, communities and cultures for future generations while allowing us to benefit from them today.

Choosing the future

As we will see in Chapters 8 and 9, there are places around the world where tourism has already adapted to meet the requirements of sustainable development. These examples demonstrate that tourism can provide positive benefits for both the local and global economy and need not have the negative impacts of tourism experienced elsewhere. However, some forms of tourism that claim to be sustainable, by using labels such as 'ecotourism', may in fact be far from sustainable. The need to assess different types of tourism, and identify those that make a genuine contribution to sustainable development, is just one of the issues that will be addressed in this book.

VIEWPOINT

'Although much promise initially surrounded the ecotourism concept, most ecotourism today is merely a market brand, with the same damaging characteristics. In fact, ecotourism impacts can be even more acute, due to the ecologically and culturally sensitive areas targeted.'
Ecumenical Coalition on Third World Tourism

This tourist recycling bottles in Spain shows that concern for the environment need not stop just because people are away from home.

DEBATE

Think about your last holiday. How did your accommodation, what you ate, your activities, or your behaviour, affect the people and environments that you visited?

THE GROWTH OF TOURISM

Accelerating growth

As we have seen, international tourist arrivals grew dramatically between 1950 and 2000, rising from 25 million to 698 million. And this extraordinary growth seems to be continuing. The WTO predicts that international tourist arrivals will reach 1 billion by 2010 and almost 1.6 billion by 2020.

In particular, the WTO expects tourism to grow rapidly in some of the less developed regions of the world, in Asia, Africa and the Middle East. By contrast, tourism in the more developed world, the

Tourists visiting the Great Pyramids at Giza in Egypt. Middle Eastern destinations like this are growing in popularity.

Americas and Europe (currently containing the main tourist centres), will grow much more slowly. So, what is causing this growth? And why are the centres of tourism shifting?

Greater wealth

One of the major causes of increased tourism is the greater wealth enjoyed by many people over the last few decades. For example, in the USA average incomes increased in real terms (allowing for inflation) from US$4,960 in 1970 to US$29,240 by 1998. More recently, incomes have also begun to rise rapidly in several less developed countries. In China, for example, average incomes more than doubled between 1990 and 2000. Most importantly for tourism, incomes have generally increased at a faster rate than basic living costs (housing, food, etc). This means that people have higher disposable incomes – money available for personal spending – than in the past. Many people are choosing to spend this disposable income on tourism both at home and abroad.

More time

As well as having larger incomes, a lot of people have more leisure time than in the past. Most full-time employment in developed countries today includes paid holidays (normally around three weeks per year). In addition, the working week is shorter than it used to be, with many now enjoying a full weekend free from work. There are also increasing numbers of people working part-time (especially in retail businesses) or in self-employment who are able to enjoy even more leisure time if they choose to.

FACT

Research has shown that the average British family spends almost 16 per cent of their annual income on holidays.

Activities such as water skiing (here in Porto Cervo, Sardinia) are popular with today's tourists who have more leisure time than they used to.

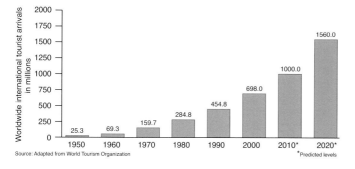

Worldwide international tourist arrivals in millions

- 1950: 25.3
- 1960: 69.3
- 1970: 159.7
- 1980: 284.8
- 1990: 454.8
- 2000: 698.0
- 2010*: 1000.0
- 2020*: 1560.0

Source: Adapted from World Tourism Organization

*Predicted levels

Retired people have more leisure time than any group in society. As they live longer and stay healthier, people in their sixties and seventies are now enjoying more active lifestyles which often include a great deal of travel and tourism.

Retired people make up a growing proportion of the world's tourists, as many of them live longer and healthier lives than in previous generations.

Freedom to move

Mobility has been central to the growth in tourism over the last fifty years. Cars and buses have become more efficient, faster and more comfortable. Improved road networks make it easier for people to travel long distances in a relatively short time, and new roads have opened up previously inaccessible areas to tourism. Such changes allow people to travel several hundred kilometres for a weekend break or even a day trip. This type of tourism plays a significant part in the economies of many developed countries. In the UK, for example, day trip spending accounted for 45 per cent of all tourism income (including from abroad) in 2001.

Shrinking the world!

Perhaps the most significant boost to tourism has been the development of low-cost, long-distance air travel. This allows previously distant locations to be reached in ever-shorter times. In 1934, for instance, a flight from London to Bangkok in

FACT

In 2000, forecasts suggested that air traffic would double by 2015 and treble by 2020. Tourists currently account for around 57 per cent of international air passengers.

Thailand took eight days and involved no fewer than sixteen stops in between! By 2002 the same flight could be made directly in only ten hours.

It is not only travelling time that has been reduced. As aircraft have been designed to carry more and more passengers, the cost of air travel has also fallen dramatically. For instance, the 1934 flight from London to Bangkok carried just eleven passengers who each paid the modern equivalent of almost £8,000. By 2002, long-distance aircraft typically carried around 380 people and the cost of a London to Bangkok ticket on a scheduled airline was around £600.

Such dramatic changes have opened up new destinations to a wider cross-section of society. In addition, isolated locations are making themselves accessible by building airports in order to make money from tourism. With new super-airliners (capable of carrying over 550 passengers) being developed, it seems that air travel will continue to speed the growth of global tourism.

FACT

When JFK airport opened in New York in 1949 it handled over 18,000 flights and almost 223,000 passengers. By 2000, it handled more than 345,000 flights and 32.8 million passengers.

Runways for small planes now allow tourists to fly into many of Africa's game reserves. These tourists have flown from Nairobi, Kenya's capital, to the Masai Mara, saving a drive of almost eight hours.

FACT

In 1998, nearly 70 per cent of Internet users were said to have clicked on a travel-related website.

Bringing the world home

Television programmes, magazines and newspaper supplements bring us information about new and exciting destinations, some of which we may never have even heard of. We are given information about how to get there, what there is to do and see, where to stay, even what to eat. This type of media coverage has encouraged the rapid growth of tourism in regions such as Africa and Asia. By bringing the world into our homes, travel journalists can make distant places and people seem more familiar and give tourists the confidence to try somewhere different.

More recently, the Internet has started to play a major role, allowing travellers to explore a chosen destination on their computers before deciding to make a booking. In fact some websites are so sophisticated that tourists may wonder whether there is anything left to see once they get there!

The Internet has become a major source of information for tourists who are planning a holiday or day out.

weblinks

For an example of on-line tourism information visit
www.waylinks.co.uk/series/
21debates/tourism

At home in the world

Modern tourism often attempts to create a sense of comfort and familiarity, both before the traveller books the trip and after he or she arrives at the destination. Everything, from food and drinks to furnishings and souvenirs, can be designed to make the tourist feel at home. In fact some hotel chains follow such a set pattern of food and furnishings in their hotels throughout the world, that – until you step beyond the hotel perimeter – you could be almost anywhere. Many people are highly critical of this type of tourism but it has been central to the growth of 'exotic' or 'far and away' resorts, as the holiday brochures like to call them.

A world of choice

Today there are endless choices, not only in terms of destination but also in the type of holiday available. This choice, catering for all tastes and markets, has further encouraged the growth of tourism in recent years. Whether tourists want to trek across the Sahara desert, lounge on a Mediterranean beach, visit remote African cultures or shop in a mega city such as Tokyo or New York, there is a company offering the holiday of their choice.

DEBATE

Think about the growth of tourism over the last fifty years. What aspects of its growth might cause most problems for the countries visited? How might tourism affect those countries, culturally, economically and environmentally?

Mega cities, such as New York in the USA, have become key tourist destinations owing to their exciting mix of history, culture, entertainment and shopping.

TYPES OF TOURISM

Package holidays

The sudden increase in tourism from 1970 onwards (see chart on page 9) can be directly linked to the rise of a particular type of tourism – package holidays. These often include flights, transfers, car hire, accommodation, food, insurance, excursions and even entertainment. They can be bought 'off the shelf' from most high street travel agents, and the most popular destinations are beach resorts.

Since their origin in the 1950s, package holidays have become a mainstay of modern tourism and some locations have thrived on offering little else. Benidorm in Spain, for example, has been transformed from a quiet seaside fishing town into a mass of hotel blocks, clubs, restaurants and bars. Its resident population of 62,000 plays host to over 5.5 million visitors a year, nearly all of them on package tours, with 1.2 million from the UK alone.

A crowded sandy beach, surrounded by hotels and apartments, at a popular Spanish resort.

Package holidays still dominate the international tourist market, but in recent years this situation has begun to change. This is partly because low-cost air travel and the development of the Internet have made it easier for people to book their own holidays. There has also been a shift in the type of tourist experience that people want.

The thrill of adventure

Adventure tourism has grown rapidly in many countries, especially among younger generations. River rafting, mountain trekking, ocean diving, desert crossings and overland tours are all possibilities open to tourists today. For example, thousands of tourists travel each year to Victoria Falls, between Zambia and Zimbabwe, where they can bungee jump from a railway bridge crossing, 111 metres into the Zambezi gorge below or go white water rafting on the Zambezi itself. Rafting is also a popular tourist attraction in the USA, Nepal, Ethiopia, Turkey, New Zealand, and Uganda where, just two years after its introduction in 1996 it had become the country's leading tourist activity.

VIEWPOINT

'The economy is good, and more and more people are willing to leave the Club Med experience for something more challenging.'
Brian Obrecht, co-founder of Outer Edge Expeditions in Walled Lake, Michigan, USA

Though popular, adventure tourism can be very disruptive. In the Himalayas, for example, litter from mountain trekkers has become a major problem, while in the Red Sea off Egypt and Israel, up to 10 per cent of the coral reef has been damaged by tourist dives.

Tourists seeking adventure raft the Nile river near its source in Uganda, East Africa.

VIEWPOINT

'Most Kenyans never go to a game park because they can't afford it. Most Kenyans have never seen a lion or an elephant.'
Anne Loehr, Director of Eco-resorts, Kenya

Nature tourism

In a world where the human population has more than doubled since 1950, natural environments have been in rapid decline. By the mid-1990s, for instance, 80 per cent of the Earth's original forest cover had been cleared or degraded. Perhaps partly because of this decline, increasing numbers of people are expressing a desire to visit the world's remaining natural or wilderness areas. Nature tourism, as it is known, is therefore becoming very popular, ranging from safaris in Africa to ocean cruises in the Antarctic.

Natural areas, like Lake Louise, Banff, in the Canadian Rockies, shown here, attract many tourists.

FACT

The USA's 384 national parks received over 424 million visitors in 2001.

Surveys suggest that around half of all tourists would like to visit unspoiled natural areas during their stay and that up to 40 per cent travel specifically to see wildlife such as birds, whales or game. Some forms of nature tourism have become very expensive, however, meaning that only the wealthy can afford them. In Uganda, for example, tourists pay around US$250 per day for a chance to see its rare mountain gorilla population.

Like adventure tourism, nature tourism is not always beneficial to local people or the environment. In Kenya, for instance, people have been displaced to make way for expensive wildlife parks which attract tourists. In many countries, however, there are natural areas that can be enjoyed free of charge. In the UK, for example, the Peak District National Park welcomes an estimated 30 million visitors a year, none of whom pay for access to the park itself.

FACT

Nature-based tourism in South Africa increased by almost 500 per cent during the 1990s to over 6 million tourists by 1999.

Theme park tourism

Over the last fifty years, theme park tourism, based around a specific attraction, has grown rapidly. The Disney resorts in the USA, France and Japan are perhaps the most famous examples of theme park tourism, but they are by no means alone. In Denmark, for example, the Legoland Park is a major tourist attraction. And in the UK, Blackpool Pleasure Beach and Alton Towers Theme Park remain among the most popular visitor attractions, clocking up over 9 million visitors between them in 2000. New theme park resorts are planned in China and Malaysia, making this type of holiday more accessible to people in South-East Asia.

weblinks

For more information on national parks in the USA go to www.waylinks.co.uk/series/21debates/tourism

The Legoland theme park is one of Denmark's top tourist attractions. Similar theme parks are now found in many tourist destinations.

Tourist attractions

Tourist attractions include historic sites, museums, gardens, educational or specialist visitor

attractions, and even whole towns and villages. Some of these attract millions of visitors each year. In the UK, for example, Stratford-upon-Avon, famous as Shakespeare's home town, is the second most popular tourist location after London, attracting nearly 4 million people a year. Meanwhile in Paris, France, the Louvre art gallery attracts 5 million people annually, and in Memphis, USA, Gracelands – the home of Elvis Presley – is visited by over a million tourists each year.

Famous people can generate a great deal of tourism interest. These tourists are visiting 'Gracelands' in Tennessee, USA, the home of rock and roll star Elvis Presley.

City breaks

As people in the developed world have gained more leisure time and higher incomes in recent years, city breaks have become an increasingly popular form of tourism. Short trips have been encouraged by reductions in air fares which make travelling between key cities easier and cheaper than ever before. European cities, such as Barcelona, Amsterdam, Paris, London, Edinburgh, Dublin and Prague, are relatively close to each other and have all benefited from this form of tourism.

Long-distance city breaks are also growing in popularity, with many people travelling from Europe to New York for a long weekend of shopping and entertainment, for example. City breaks will probably continue to grow in popularity as flights become ever cheaper. However, as short-haul flights are extremely polluting, this trend also presents some serious environmental problems (see pages 26-27).

Independent tourism

An increasing number of tourists are travelling independently. Perhaps the best known of these are the so-called 'backpackers' or 'travellers' who may travel for several months at a time, to numerous destinations. In reality, though, more and more people (not just backpackers) are taking advantage of the information and technology now available, to organize their own tourist experiences. Such tourism, usually involving individuals and small groups, is often thought to put less pressure on destinations than large-scale organized tours. However, in some cases independent tourism can be more damaging. For example, many independent travellers follow the same route, using the same guide book. This can cause problems for local communities, such as the Karen people of northern Thailand whose lifestyle is constantly disrupted by a stream of inquisitive, camera-wielding backpackers.

Backpackers wait for transport in Bangkok, Thailand. Although travelling independently, many will follow the same route and visit the same places.

DEBATE

Which types of tourism do you think have the greatest impact on people and environments and which have the least? What are your reasons?

PATTERNS OF TOURISM

FACT

Of the top forty tourist destinations in 1998, eleven were poor, less developed countries, which included China and Mexico.

weblinks

For more information about tourism and development go to www.waylinks.co.uk/series/21debates/tourism

Tourist souvenirs can provide a valuable income for local people such as these Masai in Kenya.

An uneven business

Although tourism is a global industry, it is definitely concentrated in the more developed regions of the world. In 2000, for instance, Europe accounted for nearly 58 per cent of the world's international tourist arrivals. By contrast, less than 8 per cent of international tourists visited South Asia, the Middle East and Africa combined.

Within regions, the trends can be very uneven too. For example, of the 129 million international tourists arriving in the Americas in 2000, about 40 per cent went to the USA, compared to 16 per cent who visited Mexico, and just 4 per cent who went to Brazil. Similar patterns, revealing dominant countries, are found in all regions except Europe where international arrivals are more evenly distributed.

Tourism for development

Tourism is often considered beneficial to less developed countries. Tourists bring valued foreign currency into the economy and their stay may encourage growth in the wider economy through 'knock-on' or 'multiplier' effects. For instance, tourist arrivals lead to a demand for other services and goods, such as transport, restaurants and souvenirs, which can be provided by local companies and individuals. Evidence also suggests that tourism can especially benefit women (often the poorest members of society in less developed countries) through the creation of new jobs and business opportunities.

Since 1990, the number of tourists visiting less developed regions has grown by an average of 9.5 per cent per year, compared to the world average of 4.6 per cent. The challenge ahead is to make tourism growth benefit these developing countries more.

In the past, tourism growth has sometimes led to increased crime and even riots as local residents express resentment at their land and resources being used for tourism. There is now growing pressure to make sure that local people, particularly the poor, benefit from tourism activities. 'Community tourism' and 'pro-poor tourism' projects have been started in many countries to try to achieve these aims. However, at present, many of the benefits of tourism in developing countries continue to be enjoyed by a wealthy minority or by the foreign owners of international hotel and restaurant chains.

VIEWPOINTS

'Tourism is a massive and growing industry already affecting millions of the poor, so a marginal improvement could generate substantial benefits'
UK Department for International Development (DFID), 1999

'In those places where the poor feel that they are not benefiting sufficiently or fairly from tourism, conflicts and violence can arise.'
Pro-Poor Tourism, Briefing No. 2, 2002

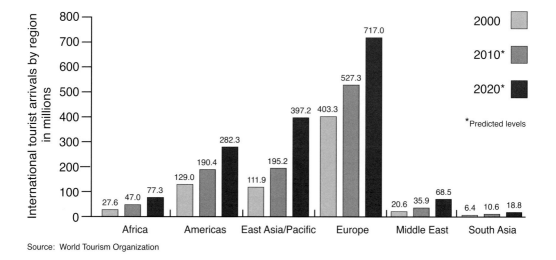

Source: World Tourism Organization

FACT

In the late 1990s, the USA, Canada, Japan and seventeen European nations accounted for around 80 per cent of tourism expenditure.

Tourist origins

Although they may be receiving more tourists than they used to, people from less developed countries still only account for a small proportion of international tourists. The majority (58.5 per cent) of visitors come from Europe, with German, British and French tourists being the most numerous. A further 19 per cent of the world's tourists come from the Americas, most of them from the USA or Canada. Tourists from the USA are also the biggest spenders. In 2000, they spent an incredible US$65 billion on international tourism – nearly 14 per cent of the world total.

Meanwhile, in 2000, fewer than 5 per cent of international tourists came from the less developed regions of Africa, the Middle East and South Asia. However, East Asia and the Pacific region (including China and Japan) are rapidly becoming major tourism centres. Not only are they the fastest-growing regions for tourist arrivals, but their populations are also travelling more. South Koreans, for example, increased their spending on international tourism by 60 per cent in 1999-2000. This meant that South Korea joined Japan and China as the third country from Asia to be among the world's top fifteen tourism spenders.

China is expected to become the world's top tourist destination by 2020. Tiananmen Square, in the capital Beijing, is a 'must-see' sight for most visitors.

The Chinese are travelling in ever greater numbers. These tourists are visiting the Eiffel Tower in Paris, France – the world's number one tourist destination in 2002.

An elite club?

With tourist arrivals, origins and spending all dominated by a few developed countries, it is not surprising that some critics have accused the tourist industry of being an elite club. They claim that only wealthy people from the developed world are able to enjoy tourism. For people from poorer countries, the benefits of international tourism remain out of reach – as they were for many Europeans in the first half of the twentieth century.

If less developed countries wish to become international tourist destinations, they need to provide the quality of transport, accommodation and food that most tourists have come to expect. Foreign companies are often invited to provide such facilities, but this results in much of the income from tourism 'leaking' back out of the country as payment for goods and services or as profit taken out by the investing companies. In the Caribbean Islands, for example, between 50 and 70 per cent of tourism earnings 'leak out' in this way.

VIEWPOINT

'Many hotels and businesses in the developing world rely heavily on foreign inputs either because the host country lacks the luxury goods and services that many tourists demand or because ... it is difficult to procure [get] local supplies'
Lisa Mastny, WorldWatch Institute, 2002

Foreign tour operators based in developed countries have often been accused of exploiting host nations to benefit their own businesses. Campaigners believe that hosts should receive a fairer share of the profits from tourism based in their country and that 'leakage' should be reduced to a minimum. Many tour operators claim that they could not continue to operate under such conditions, but examples from around the world demonstrate that it is possible for both foreign businesses and local communities to benefit from tourism.

Emerging patterns

As travel becomes easier and cheaper, alternative patterns of tourism are emerging based on individuals planning their own holidays. However, because guide books often focus on the same few countries and destinations, many of these tourists are doing little more than creating a new form of package tourism. In more unusual tourist destinations, such as Uganda in East Africa, independent travellers all tend to follow the same well-trodden route around the country, using their trusted guide books. The same few hotels, restaurants and attractions will benefit, but – as with other forms of tourism – many areas and communities are ignored.

weblinks

For more information on responsible tourism and the environment go to www.waylinks.co.uk/series/21debates/tourism

Some independent travellers do venture 'off the beaten track' and visit new areas but, while this might help to spread the economic benefits of tourism, it can also lead to problems. One of the greatest concerns is that, in areas with little existing tourism, there is no regulation of tourist activities, and visitor numbers may increase unchecked. This could lead to environmental damage and disruption of local cultures. Even where regulations do exist they are often only weakly upheld.

VIEWPOINT

'Support the local economy by using locally owned restaurants and hotels, buying local products made by locals from renewable resources.'
Partners in Responsible Tourism

As the impact of tourism on people and environments has been publicized through the media and various campaign groups, there has been a growing demand for more responsible forms of tourism. These would show greater respect for local people and their environments and attempt to minimize the impact of tourism. More responsible tourism should also ensure that local communities benefit from the income generated by tourism and that the profits should not simply be taken out of the country by foreign companies. There is growing evidence that tourists around the world are willing to pay more for holidays that reflect the principles of responsible tourism. The challenge, in such an unregulated industry, is to find out which holidays and tour operators truly follow these principles.

Tourists get 'off the beaten track' in the Annapurna foothills of Nepal. The benefits of such tourism – for local people and environments – are questionable.

DEBATE

Who will benefit the most from the changing patterns and trends in international tourism? What might be done to improve the benefits for less developed regions of the world?

TOURISM AND THE ENVIRONMENT

weblinks

To find out how polluting international air travel can be, go to www.waylinks.co.uk/series/21debates/tourism

A dirty business

Tourism's environmental impact begins from the moment people begin their trip. Up to 90 per cent of the energy consumed by tourists is used in getting to and from their destination. This energy, most of it from oil, produces vast quantities of air pollution. And the environmental impact does not stop when the tourists arrive at their holiday destination. The fuel, food, water and accommodation that they enjoy all have an impact on the environment. And then there is the waste they produce from left-over food, sewage, and general litter. Tourist activities, such as safari drives, coral diving and even swimming in a hotel pool, also have environmental impacts. In short, tourism can be quite a dirty business and the tourist industry is now under enormous pressure, from environmental groups, local residents and tourists themselves, to clean up its act.

Air transport and global warming

Air transport has become the most popular method of travel for international tourists, accounting for 43 per cent of tourist travel. With increasing numbers expected to travel by air in future, considerable attention is being focused on the environmental costs of flying.

Aircraft produce a relatively small 3.5 per cent of greenhouse gas emissions from human sources. However they are the main source of greenhouse gases released into the upper atmosphere, and scientists have shown that gases released at this level have a greater warming effect on climate than those released at ground level.

Experts expect the share of greenhouse gas emissions from aircraft to increase by up to four times by 2050, even allowing for improvements in fuel efficiency and aircraft design. The warming effect of these emissions could have significant impacts, including – ironically – destroying a number of tourist destinations. In the most severe cases, rising sea levels may lead to some resorts, such as low-lying Pacific islands, disappearing altogether. The popular Maldives in the Indian Ocean are especially at risk if current trends continue.

FACT

The fuel efficiency of aircraft doubled between 1970 and 2000 and it is expected to improve further in future.

In other countries climatic changes may result in extreme conditions such as heat waves, drought or flooding that will deter tourists from visiting. There is also concern about warmer temperatures leading to the spread of tropical diseases such as malaria.

The stunning Maldive Islands are less than 2 metres above sea level. If global warming causes sea levels to rise as expected, they could be submerged by 2030.

FACT

Cruise tourism is expected to grow from nearly 10 million annual passengers in 2000 to almost 21 million passengers a year by 2010.

Floating hazards

One of the fastest-growing forms of tourism is cruising. The number of cruise tourists doubled during the 1990s, reaching almost 10 million annual passengers by 2000. Cruise ships resemble water-borne mini-cities and they have a very poor environmental record. As their popularity continues to grow, they present an increasing threat to the world's marine environments. The Bluewater Network, which campaigns to clean up the cruise industry, claims that a typical one-week cruise generates around 50 tonnes of rubbish, 9 million litres of "graywater" (waste water from sinks, showers, galleys and laundry), 955,000 litres of sewage, 160,000 litres of oil-contaminated water, and large volumes of hazardous waste such as chemicals from on-board photograph-processing services.

The popularity of cruises has led to damage around many ports and harbours. These cruise liners are moored at Nassau in the Bahamas.

On older ships much of this waste is dumped overboard where it can cause serious harm. Newer vessels, in contrast, have treatment and storage facilities, allowing them to transfer waste to shore when they reach port. But, despite such improvements, campaigners claim that a great deal of waste is illegally dumped by the cruise industry. Between 1993 and 1998, there were 104 cases where ships were caught and fined a total of US$30 million for the illegal dumping of waste.

Cruise ships can also harm the environment when they dock in port. In the Cayman Islands, for example, sizeable areas of coral have been destroyed around the harbour of Georgetown by large ships anchoring. In other areas where the local communities are keen to benefit from tourist spending, channels have been dredged and coastlines altered to allow cruise ships to visit. However such alterations have frequently caused enormous damage to coastal ecosystems.

Land clearance

All over the world, vast areas of land have been cleared to make way for the massive growth of tourism in the last thirty years. This clearance is not just to build hotels and holiday apartments but also to provide airports, roads, shops and leisure facilities such as golf courses and casinos.

Unfortunately today's tourists are increasingly attracted to areas that are not only beautiful but also environmentally sensitive. Coral reefs, rainforests, savannah grasslands, mountains and tropical beaches are among the richest ecosystems in the world and contain many of its most endangered species. As tourism in these areas develops, these finely balanced ecosystems are often put under enormous pressure.

FACT

An estimated 77 per cent of all ship waste comes from cruise liners.

VIEWPOINTS

'Although the industry's continued success ultimately depends on the beauty of the oceans, the armada of cruise ships now plying the planet's waters trails behind it a wake of pollution.'
Kira Schmidt. Campaign Director. Bluewater Network

'Royal Caribbean International and Celebrity Cruises has established an officer position on its ships to solely focus on environmental programs and compliance with the international and US environment protection regulations.'
Royal Caribbean Cruises website

FACT

In Grenada tourists use about seven times as much water as local people and they are even given priority for water supply during droughts.

There are many examples of ecosystems being damaged by tourism. In the Caribbean, for example, wetlands have been dredged and filled and sand dunes mined to make way for coastal tourist resorts. This has resulted in a decline in local fish species and the choking of coral reefs – the very attractions that many tourists come to see! Similar destruction of coastal environments has occurred in other tropical destinations such as Mexico, where 65 per cent of the country's mangrove swamps have already been lost, and Kenya, where coral reefs are highly threatened by tourism, fishing and other human activities.

Resource competition

Tourists use large quantities of natural resources and in some regions this is threatening local environments and the livelihoods of local people. In the Philippines, for instance, the famous 3,000-year-old Ifugao rice terraces in Banaue, visited by many tourists and sometimes described as the 'Eighth Wonder of the World', are beginning to dry

The world-famous Ifugao rice terraces of the Philippines are now under threat from the tourism industry that has made them so popular.

up, owing to the extraction of water for new tourist hotels. Many farmers have abandoned their plots and other plots are falling into disrepair. At the same time, elsewhere in the Philippines trees are being cut down to make carvings and other tourist souvenirs, destroying forest resources.

Using water for tourism facilities, such as golf courses and swimming pools, has caused problems throughout the world. In Israel, for example, water levels in the Dead Sea have fallen by over 40 metres in the last fifty years due to tourism demands. At present rates, experts predict the Dead Sea could dry up completely by 2050. Meanwhile, in one area of Kenya, the Samburu people have been forced to find new watering holes for their livestock as water is diverted to fill swimming pools in a nearby tourist lodge.

VIEWPOINTS

'We cannot just stop the livelihood of the woodcarvers [of Ifugao]. Neither can we stop the tourism industry.'
Juan Dait, Jr., Executive Director, Ifugao Terraces Commission [ITC]

'Eventually, the very reason that made the tourism industry flourish in Ifugao will be gone forever, driving the tourists away, and leaving the people with whatever is left of their culture, environment and dignity'
Wilfredo Alangui, Tebtebba Foundation, Philippines

Floating in the unique waters of the Dead Sea in Israel could soon become a tourist attraction of the past due to water extraction.

In less developed countries woodland is often cleared to provide fuel or construction materials for tourist lodges and hotels. In Kenya, Nepal and Tanzania, this has meant that local people have had to travel further to source their own fuel wood, leading to greater erosion as tree cover is reduced. Some lodges have now recognized this problem. In Kenya's Amboseli National Park, for example, two tour companies invite visitors to plant a tree when they check in, as part of a plan to reforest the park.

VIEWPOINT

'Fifteen years ago, divers and dive operators thought nothing of breaking off a piece of coral as a souvenir. Today, 99.9% would never think of doing that.'

Jeff Nadler, Professional Association of Dive Instructors (PADI)

Wildlife impacts

Wildlife is a major tourist attraction, but in many destinations animal numbers and behavioural patterns have changed as a result of tourism. For example, in Africa's wildlife parks predators such as lions, leopards and cheetahs have changed their breeding and hunting patterns owing to the hundreds of tourist vehicles that constantly pursue them. Cheetahs now hunt in the middle of the day when there are fewer tourists around, but the heat at that time means that fewer of their hunts are successful and their cubs are increasingly going hungry.

Wildlife tourism, here in Kenya, has a mixed impact on the environment.

weblinks

To find out more about tourism, wildlife and the environment visit www.waylinks.co.uk/series/ 21debates/tourism

In Alaska endangered humpback whales have been hit and killed by the growing numbers of cruise boats in the region; and in Western Australia's Shark Bay dolphins have become so used to tourists that they now appear each day to be fed and petted. In Grand Cayman, in the Caribbean, sting rays have become so accustomed to being fed by tourists that divers without food for them have been attacked by the disappointed rays.

Besides changes to animal behaviour, habitats can also be drastically affected by wildlife tourism. For example, in Kenya's Masai Mara the number of tourist vehicles increased from 20,000 in 1986 to over 60,000 by 1998, leading to rapid soil erosion and habitat destruction. In Yellowstone and Grand Teton National Parks in the USA, the use of snowmobiles during the winter months is to be regulated from 2003-4 because of the harm done to wildlife and the noise of the vehicles. Multi-passenger snowcoaches will be introduced, to allow the public continued access to the parks.

Despite the potential problems of wildlife tourism, it can, if properly managed, benefit wildlife by raising awareness and generating income to help conserve natural habitats. In Uganda, for instance, the fees paid by people visiting the country's mountain gorillas provide around 70 per cent of the funds needed to maintain the country's other eleven national parks. By keeping the number of visitors low, the park authorities can also make sure that tourists do not disturb the gorillas' natural behaviour or environment.

VIEWPOINTS

'Unfortunately, snowmobiles have been shown to harm wildlife, air quality and the natural quiet of these parks.'
Karen Wade, Intermountain Regional Director, US National Park Service

'Scientific data now show that snowmobiles do not significantly impact the environment when driven on snow-covered groomed roads in managed sections of Yellowstone and Grand Teton.'
Ed Klim, President of International Snowmobile Manufacturers Association (ISMA)

The endangered mountain gorillas of Uganda may become extinct without the interest and income that tourism brings.

DEBATE

On balance, do you think tourism is good or bad for the environment? What reasons can you give to support your view?

TOURISM AND CULTURE

weblinks

For more on tourism and local cultures go to
www.waylinks.co.uk/series/21debates/tourism

VIEWPOINT

'Lijiang's Naxi seem often marginalized as players in a cultural theme park'
The Rough Guide to China, 2000

Don't forget us!

Tourism often bypasses local communities in terms of economic benefits, while the big profits are made by foreign hotel chain owners or tour operators. Local people are also frequently ignored in other ways. For example, though there is much concern about tourism's environmental impact, there is much less anxiety about its influence on local people and cultures. As demand for more responsible forms of tourism has grown, however, local cultures are at last being considered. Some are even benefiting from the changing trends in the industry.

Cultural exhibitionism

People and their cultures have themselves become tourist attractions in many countries. In China, for example, thousands of tourists descend on the town of Lijiang each year to visit the remote Naxi people and their ancient culture. This has been actively promoted by the Chinese government as part of its tourism drive (China is set to become the world's number one tourist destination by 2020), but critics are concerned that the Naxi will be reduced to little more than a commercial tourist exhibit.

The Naxi of China are promoted as a cultural tourist attraction, but there are serious questions about who benefits most from such tourism.

These Masai in Kenya perform a dance show for tourists staying in one of the Masai Mara's luxury tented camps. Some people believe that such shows help to preserve local traditions.

This has certainly happened among other communities such as the Masai in Kenya. Many Masai now wait in show villages for passing tourists. There they will perform traditional dances and dress in traditional costume in order to have their photographs taken in return for money. In between performances some of them make so-called 'traditional' artefacts to sell. However, in reality these are often mass-produced to suit the tourist market and not very traditional at all.

In an extreme example of cultural exhibitionism, many Padaung women – who fled from Burma as refugees – live in camps in Thailand where tourists visit to take photographs or buy souvenirs. They are sometimes called 'giraffe women' because of the coils placed around their necks, to lengthen them, from the age of five. Traditionally only selected girls born at a certain time had their necks lengthened, but today many girls are treated in this way in order to meet the tourist demand for 'exotic sights'.

VIEWPOINTS

'Continue .... to Padong [sic] village, home of the long-necked Padong tribe (Giraffe Women), wearing brass rings around their elongated necks – an extraordinary sight.'
Promotional literature, Thai tour operator

'Maybe soon there will not be any of us left at all. My grandchildren don't want to go to school in cities where people will stare at them all the time. Before, they considered themselves special. Now they have seen many fancy things, cameras and videos and television, maybe they will not want this life any more.'
Mu Kyeh, Padaung woman

VIEWPOINTS

'As long as tourists just want a glimpse of the local atmosphere, a quick glance at local life, without any knowledge or even interest, staging [staged cultural attractions] will be inevitable.'
United Nations Environment Programme (UNEP) Tourism Programme

'What hurts Indians most is that our costumes are considered beautiful, but it's as if the person wearing it didn't exist.'
Rigoberta Menchu, Guatemalan Quiché Indian and Nobel Peace Prize winner

Preservation or exploitation?

Many tour operators claim that, without the interest of tourists, some world cultures would disappear under the pressures of modern life. This has been said of the Masai in Kenya, for example, and it is certainly true that Kenya's other tribal groups (who are of less interest to tourists) have all but lost many of their traditions. But can tourism really claim to be preserving cultures?

Many would argue that, on the contrary, tourism exploits people and their cultures for its own ends. Tourist advertisements point to the costumes, artefacts, music and dance of traditional people, but rarely offer any detailed information about their culture – their beliefs, morals and customs. In fact in some so-called 'cultural attractions' the people wearing costumes and performing for tourists may not even be from the cultural group they are representing. In such instances culture becomes little more than a 'product' that is sold to make a profit.

Gaining control

Many of the cultures that attract tourists are those of indigenous peoples, who originated in that region, such as the Aborigines in Australia or the Inuit in Canada. These peoples are often minority groups within the bigger population and they rarely have much control over tourism and its impact.

However this situation is gradually beginning to change, as in the case of the Kuna indigenous people who live on Panama's Caribbean coast – a popular tourist destination, especially for cruise ships.

An Aborigine works in the tourist industry in his native Australia.

Kuna villagers offer their souvenirs to passing cruise ships in the hope of earning some valuable tourist dollars.

Concerned about the loss of their traditional culture and the leaking of profits to outside tour companies, the Kuna passed laws in 1996 to control tourism within their lands. Limits have been placed on the number of hotels that can be built and both the hotels and the cruise ships are taxed according to the number of visitors they attract. However, despite the laws, many Kuna are attracted by the lure of tourist dollars and there is still some unofficial tourist activity. As cruise ships pass, for example, the Kuna will paddle their dugout canoes alongside to sell mass-produced souvenirs. A single cruise ship can generate up to US$10,000 worth of trade – good earnings for one of Panama's poorest communities.

FACT

Cruise tourists used to throw coins overboard to watch the Kuna dive for them. Several Kuna drowned as a result and the new tourism laws ban this practice.

VIEWPOINT

'[The Kuna] don't plant yucca, plantains or guineas anymore because they are just waiting for the cruise ship'
Anonymous Kuna member

VIEWPOINT

'...even small groups of people, or for that matter the lone traveller, no matter how sensitive, may have a disruptive effect on local culture.'
The New Imperialism, Survival International magazine

This beach on Phi Phi Le, Thailand, was at the centre of publicity surrounding a film called The Beach *in 2000.*

A day at *The Beach*

There are other powerful links between culture and tourism. For example, in 2000 the film *The Beach*, starring Leonardo DiCaprio, made Phi Phi Le, a small island off southern Thailand inside a marine national park, into one of the world's most talked-about tourist locations. Unfortunately, in this instance it was for all the wrong reasons. The film's producers had bulldozed away sand dunes and vegetation and planted sixty non-native palm trees to improve the setting for the film. Although the environment was later restored, environmentalists were furious that such actions were allowed inside a national park already threatened by the impact of tourism. Despite the controversy, its newfound fame has made Phi Phi Le even more popular as a tourist destination.

Other films and television programmes have had a similar impact on tourism in the area where they were filmed. In Melbourne, Australia, for example, the street setting of the television soap opera *Neighbours* receives thousands of visitors every year. While such interest can give the local economy a welcome boost, it can also create new pressures. For instance, some areas might be too sensitive to receive large numbers of tourists, while in others excessive interest can cause transport or accommodation problems.

In New York, there are organized tours around the city's numerous landmarks made famous in film and TV. Tourists are keen to visit the apartment block used in the TV series *Friends*, for example, or the house of the *Cosby Show* family. Such popularity can cause problems, however, as in the UK town of Holmfirth, the setting for the TV show *The Last of the Summer Wine*. So many tourists now visit the town that traffic congestion has become a major problem.

Respect and understanding

Tourism will almost always have an impact on local cultures simply because it brings people from different backgrounds together. These differences can lead to tensions, unless tourists show respect for local customs. For instance, though we may go on holiday to 'catch the sun', we need to remember that showing too much of our bodies is extremely offensive in some societies, especially Islamic ones. Similarly, some cultures believe that photographs remove people's spirits and thus do not wish to be photographed. In all these cases, tourists need to show sensitivity and respect towards their hosts in order to avoid damaging the cultures they have come to see.

FACT

Following the filming of *Lord of the Rings* in New Zealand, tourism in the country increased by 20 per cent.

— **weblinks** —

For more information about tourism impacts in less developed countries go to www.waylinks.co.uk/series/21debates/tourism

VIEWPOINT

'Cinema has probably achieved more than even the jet airliner in stimulating a taste for travel. No corner of the planet is too remote for the camera and, once a place has had a starring screen role, film fans often clamour to visit it for real.'
'On Location', Sunday Times newspaper, UK

DEBATE

Does tourism help to preserve indigenous cultures or help to destroy them?

TOURISM DEPENDENCY

A fragile living

The tourism boom has greatly benefited many countries and individual locations. It has brought new wealth and helped to develop new skills and services that are of use, not only to tourists but also to the wider community. This is particularly true in many less developed countries where tourism has made a significant contribution to economic growth. In some countries, however, there is now growing concern that their economies may be too dependent on

Rickshaw drivers wait patiently for tourists in Kolkata (formerly Calcutta), India. Such services benefit local people, but those providing the services can become too dependent on tourist income.

tourism. New consumer trends and recent world events, including terrorist attacks, diseases and natural disasters, have shown that the tourism industry can be very vulnerable to sudden change. For millions of people around the world, it could therefore prove to be a very fragile way of making a living.

A state of dependency

Many regions and countries now find themselves in a state of tourism dependency. This is particularly true of less developed countries that lack natural resources or a developed industrial sector. For such countries their attractiveness to tourists may be one of the few assets enabling them to earn valuable foreign income and support their growing economies. The World Tourism Organization (WTO) claims that tourism is the main source of foreign-exchange earnings in at least 38 per cent of the world's countries, and among the top five exports (tourism earnings are counted as export earnings) for 83 per cent.

The Caribbean is one of the most tourism-dependent regions in the world. On some of its islands, tourism provides over 30 per cent of the income and employs a quarter of the workforce. Many more people are indirectly dependent on tourism because they provide goods and services to those working in the tourist industry. This means that, should tourist numbers fall in the Caribbean, many millions of people would be affected. Similar examples of dependency are found throughout the world. For instance, African countries such as the Gambia, Egypt and Kenya have all become heavily dependent on tourism as a major contributor to their economies, and all face similar potential problems. If they are to continue to depend on tourism then such countries will need to learn to adapt quickly to the ever-changing trends in the global tourist industry.

VIEWPOINT

'...environmental shocks such as hurricanes or other natural hazards ... can quickly wipe out the progress [in tourism] built up over many years'
H.E. Carlston Boucher. Vice-Chairman. Alliance of Small Island States

In 2001 tourism in the UK was severely affected by an outbreak of foot and mouth disease that resulted in much of the countryside being closed to tourists.

Tourist shocks

Tourism has repeatedly shown itself to be vulnerable to 'shocks' such as natural hazards and diseases. Tropical countries are especially vulnerable as they suffer a higher frequency of natural events including hurricanes, and climatic extremes like droughts or flooding. In the Caribbean, for example, the islands of Antigua, Dominica, Guadeloupe and St Lucia have all had tourist facilities damaged by hurricanes in recent years. Unfortunately, media coverage of such hazards can further deter tourists and make the situation appear far worse than it is. And natural hazards are not limited to tropical countries. In 1996, over seventy people were killed and a campsite washed away during flash floods in the mountains of the Pyrenees, in Spain.

The WTO has recognized the problem of these 'shocks' and, together with the World Meteorological Organization, has developed guidelines on how countries can reduce the danger of natural hazards in order to minimize their impact on tourism. On the Indian Ocean island of Mauritius, for example, hoteliers have carefully prepared plans of what to do in the event of a cyclone. Such plans offer reassurance to tourists and significantly reduce the risk of injury or loss of life. As tourists venture into ever more remote and potentially hazardous parts of the world, providing information about the possible dangers and reducing the risks will be vital to the survival of the industry in those regions.

Safe and secure

When people travel, particularly to unfamiliar places, they like to be reassured that both they and their belongings are safe. If confidence in a particular location is shaken then tourists can very quickly look to alternative destinations. In Uganda, for instance, the tourist industry suffered a major setback in 1999 when eight European tourists were killed by rebels while they visited the country's famous mountain gorillas. Likewise, neighbouring Kenya suffered an almost 11 per cent fall in tourist visitors following political violence along its popular coastal strip during the 1997 elections.

FACT

Mount Pinatubo in the Philippines, which erupted violently in 1991, now attracts 1,000 tourists a month who come to see the devastation left behind.

For countries that are heavily dependent on tourism, making sure their guests are safe has become a major priority. In Jamaica and other Caribbean destinations, problems with crime have led companies to develop all-inclusive resorts. These are completely self-contained resorts offering everything that most holidaymakers are likely to need.

A normally popular beach at Malindi in Kenya is deserted following disturbances in the region during the 1997 elections.

weblinks

For more information about
the impact of terrorism
on tourism go to
www.waylinks.co.uk/series/
21debates/tourism

VIEWPOINT

'The aftermath of
September 11 has
shown us how
important travel and
tourism are to the
global economy, but
also how over-
dependence on tourism
can devastate lives and
derail economies.'
*Lisa Mastny, WorldWatch
Institute*

An Egyptian sells souvenirs at Khan al-Khalili. Egypt suffered a downturn in tourism following the terrorist attacks on New York in September 2001. The impact on local sellers has been significant.

All-inclusive resorts have been criticized by many who claim that they shut out local communities, creating resentment towards the tourist industry and preventing local people from benefiting through, for example, the sale of souvenirs or local foodstuffs. By fuelling such resentment, these resorts can sometimes, ironically, lead to an increase in crime levels against tourists.

Critics of all-inclusive resorts would argue that it is better and safer to involve local communities in the development of the industry. Where this has happened, and local people have experienced the benefits of tourism, security is usually a fairly minor problem.

Globally vulnerable?

International concern about tourism dependency increased dramatically in 2001 following the 11 September attack on the World Trade Center in New York. The uncertainty brought about by this terrorist attack, and the fact that commercial aircraft were used in it, made people across the world nervous about travelling and especially about flying. Tourist bookings fell throughout the world and many people cancelled their travel plans as they waited to see what would happen. The International Labour Organization estimates that up to 9 million tourist industry workers may have lost their jobs as a result of the attacks, and this does not include those outside the industry itself who are nevertheless dependent on tourism for their income because they supply goods and services to tourists and resorts. As tourists stop travelling

to places they consider dangerous and start visiting new, supposedly safer destinations, countries that have previously depended on tourist income may have to think again – at least in the short term. In Egypt, for example, tourism fell by almost 16 per cent in 2001, while in Costa Rica bookings were said to be down by 30 per cent compared with the previous year. Long-haul destinations such as these seem especially vulnerable at a time when tourists are choosing to stay closer to home and travelling by land or sea rather than by air. This change in tourism habits has also affected many of the world's major airlines who between them lost an estimated US$13 billion in 2001. Several, including Swissair and Sabena, went bankrupt.

These American tourists have decided to enjoy a hiking holiday in Mount Rainier National Park, Washington State, USA, rather than travel overseas.

DEBATE

How can a country benefit from tourism without becoming over-dependent on it? Do the short-term economic rewards outweigh the risk of a sudden drop in tourism in the future?

SUSTAINABLE TOURISM

A new direction

Many organizations and individuals (including a lot of tourists themselves) are becoming increasingly concerned about the impact of tourism – its environmental effects, its sometimes damaging effects on local cultures, and the economic risks posed to countries that become too dependent on the tourist industry. We have seen some of the issues raised by these different concerns in the last three chapters, but how is it possible to deal with them all together? In truth this is by no means a simple task. But, as we enter the twenty-first century, a new direction in tourism is slowly emerging and it has been given a name – 'sustainable tourism'.

What is sustainable tourism?

Sustainable tourism follows the principles of sustainable development – that we should only use resources in ways that do not diminish or damage them in the long term. This means that tourism activities should aim to provide economic and social benefits, but in a manner that protects local cultures and the environment for the benefit of future generations.

At present, there are very few examples of tourism that fulfil all these aims, but there are signs that the industry is beginning to take issues of sustainability seriously. This is partly because their customers, tourists themselves, are demanding a more environmentally and socially friendly form of tourism. Studies in the USA and UK, for example, have shown that people are increasingly looking for holiday and travel services that take greater account of protecting the environment.

This Kenyan resort is using renewable and sustainable solar energy to provide its own electricity.

The Eden Project in Cornwall, UK, demonstrates the importance of natural environments. It has become a major tourist attraction since it opened in 2000.

weblinks

For more information about sustainable tourism go to www.waylinks.co.uk/series/21debates/tourism

VIEWPOINTS

'Putting tourism on a sustainable path is a major challenge, but one that also presents a significant opportunity'
Klaus Topfer, Executive Director, United Nations Environment Programme (UNEP)

'The mass tourism operators have learnt the language of sustainable tourism, or whatever you want to call it, but little has really changed.'
Patricia Barnett, Director, Tourism Concern

More than words!

Some travel companies appear to see their customers' concerns simply as a marketing opportunity, often using language and words suggesting that they offer 'sustainable holidays' when in fact little may have changed. The 'eco' label is a case in point, with 'ecotourism' becoming increasingly popular among holiday-makers. Other descriptions, such as 'community-based tourism', 'responsible tourism', 'green tourism' and indeed 'sustainable tourism', are also becoming common in tourism advertisements and promotional literature. Using these words is easy, but turning them into a reality is much more complex!

Making tourism 'eco'

Ecotourism has become such a well-known term that the United Nations (UN) declared 2002 the International Year of Ecotourism (IYE). While the UN promoted this as a positive turning point for international tourism, many people and organizations have been less welcoming. They are concerned that powerful transnational companies will use the IYE to their own advantage and that it will simply become another form of mass tourism under a new label. They argue that many of the areas currently undisturbed by tourism could find themselves the target of new developments that, while 'eco' in name, are not always very 'eco' in nature. In South-East Asia, for example, there are so-called ecotourism developments underway that involve clearing large areas (including tropical forests and national parks) and moving thousands of local people away from their traditional lands. Critics of the IYE say that holiday operators need to learn from the past successes and failures of ecotourism before it is promoted worldwide.

Ecotourists search the rainforest canopy in Ecuador for signs of the wildlife that many of them have come to see.

Small is beautiful

The idea of ecotourism is not new. In the US Virgin Islands, for example, resorts constructed using recycled building materials, powered by solar energy, and offering locally produced food, have been in operation for over twenty-five years. And in the Maldives laws dating back to 1979 have ensured that the local community benefits financially from tourism in their lands, and that local resources, such as water and trees, are not harmed in any way. The development of new resorts in the Maldives is strictly managed and, even in the most luxurious developments, environmental concerns come first.

VIEWPOINT

'To ensure that ecotourism follows a truly sustainable path will require increased cooperation – and partnerships – among the tourism industry, governments, local people and the tourists themselves.'
Klaus Toepfer, Executive Director, United Nations Environment Programme

FACT

As many as 90 per cent of the hotels and restaurants along the coastal strip of Belize are now owned by foreign investors.

Developments such as these holiday homes being built in Caulkers Cay, Belize, can destroy local habitats and disrupt or displace local people.

The key to success with such resorts seems to be to limit their size and to restrict the number of visitors. This ensures that the environmental impact is minimal and local communities benefit without too much disruption to their lives. When ecotourism projects are developed on a bigger scale, however, they often cause problems. In Belize, for example, American developers have moved in to take advantage of the country's ecotourism boom, buying up land and preventing local people from using resources for their own livelihoods and development.

weblinks

For more information and debate about ecotourism go to
www.waylinks.co.uk/series/
21debates/tourism

VIEWPOINT

'Our goal is to be one of the most environmentally friendly companies in the hotel industry and to conduct our business on nature's terms.'
Scandic Hotels. Sweden. Environmental Policy

Learning from success

One important move towards more environment-friendly tourism was the establishment of the International Hotels Environment Initiative (IHEI) in 1992. The IHEI advises hotels, suppliers, tourist authorities and others on how to fulfil their environmental and social responsibilities. In early 2002, around 11,200 hotels were members of IHEI, representing roughly 2 million hotel rooms across five continents. Many of these hotels have adopted simple measures such as providing room cards that encourage guests only to have their towels and linen washed when necessary and not every day. Studies have shown that this can save the equivalent of 114 litres of water per room per day and reduce other costs by around 20 per cent.

Some individual hotel chains are going even further. For instance, Scandic Hotels of Sweden have introduced new 'environmental rooms'. The materials used to construct and furnish the rooms are nearly all natural, biodegradable or recycled. Although costing 10 per cent more per room to build, the environmental rooms have proven popular with customers and are always the first to be booked.

On a different issue, the African country of Namibia has attracted worldwide attention for its success in giving greater control of tourism to local communities. These communities have been given the right to set up their own tourist zones and develop attractions, campsites or lodges, as they wish. They have also formed an organization – Namibia Community Based Tourism Association (NACOBTA) – to provide business training for community members and help market their attractions internationally. The scheme generates profits which benefit the whole community and not just those directly involved with tourism.

FACT

In 2002 there were over 100 tourism certification schemes around the world, but no internationally agreed system.

Sussusvlei Karos Lodge in Namibia is a locally run tourist lodge that benefits the Namibian communities living nearby. Such locally managed resorts can bring significant benefits to poorer communities.

Making it clear

For tourists looking for more environment-friendly holiday options, finding accurate and reliable information can be difficult. With so many different terms being used, and few regulations, companies have been able to make all sorts of groundless claims about the holidays they offer. Thankfully this is now changing as a number of schemes around the world introduce certificates or ratings to advise customers of how sustainable a particular hotel, resort or company is. Australia has led the way with this approach, introducing the National Ecotourism Accreditation Programme (NEAP) in 1996. To qualify, hotels, resorts and holiday packages must meet several environmental, social and cultural standards.

The wildlife of the Galapagos Islands (much of which is unique) is protected by limits on tourist numbers and activities.

VIEWPOINTS

'From multinational luxury chains to three-room jungle lodges, hotels are cashing in on the eco-trend. They're recycling, asking guests to reuse towels, and spending thousands of dollars on getting eco-certified'
Paula Szuchman, Condé Nast Traveler *magazine*

'If an [ecotourism] accreditation scheme is going to work it needs to be globally effective'
Steve Watkins, Geographical *Magazine*

A number of hotel certification schemes also exist, such as the international ECOTEL certificate or the Certificate for Sustainable Tourism in Costa Rica. These rank hotels (normally on a scale of 1 to 5) on the basis of their environmental and social responsibility. In the Galapagos Islands a 'SmartVoyager' certificate is awarded to visiting ships and tour operators that comply with local regulations to protect the islands' unique environment. The Galapagos Islands are home to wildlife found nowhere else in the world, but this makes them of great interest to tourists and brings many associated problems. The SmartVoyager scheme is intended to control tourism in the islands. The awards from such groups have become highly sought-after and are not easy to achieve. ECOTEL, for example, has certified only forty-one hotels worldwide, from over 1,000 applications, since it began in 1994.

The challenge ahead is for the different elements of the tourist industry to come together and agree an international scheme for accrediting genuinely sustainable, environment-friendly tourist products. This will make it easier for tourists to make properly informed decisions and harder for tour companies and hotels to make false claims.

Paying the price

Tourists will also have to be prepared to pay higher prices for sustainable tourism. In surveys tourists often say that they are willing to pay extra for a more sustainable holiday, but the reality can be quite different. Many forms of sustainable tourism are already more expensive because they are based on smaller numbers of visitors. In the fragile South-East Asian mountain kingdom of Bhutan, for example, tourism is limited to less than 10,000 tourists a year to keep the industry sustainable, with each visitor paying around US$250 per day.

The remote mountain kingdom of Bhutan has strict limits on tourism to help conserve the environment and the local way of life.

Making the mainstream tourism industry pay for sustainability is more complicated, but several schemes are now either on trial or in operation. At Luton Airport in the UK, for instance, travellers are invited to pay a voluntary 'Green Tax' to account for the carbon dioxide emitted by their journey. The charge of 0.2 pence per mile is used to fund a local tree-planting scheme to help absorb the carbon dioxide emitted by the aviation industry.

weblinks

For information about
the International
Ecotourism Society go to
www.waylinks.co.uk/series/
21debates/tourism

In May 2002 a compulsory 'eco tax' was introduced on visitors staying in Spain's Balearic Islands' hotels. The islands, which include Ibiza, Majorca and Minorca, attract over 10 million tourists a year, causing a lot of damage to the environment. The funds raised by the tax will go towards environmental improvements and new projects such as cycle paths. Some hotel owners have objected to the tax of 1 euro per person per night, claiming that it will stop tourists visiting the islands. Similar taxes introduced in the Seychelles were reduced and later abolished in 2000 under pressure from tour operators.

What can tourists do?

There are many ways in which tourists themselves can help create a more sustainable tourist industry. Paying eco taxes or voluntary charges is one way of helping, but behaviour and attitudes also make a difference. For instance, by finding out more about a destination before booking a holiday, tourists can reduce their impact on local cultures while they are there. They can ask questions of tour operators and airlines in order to decide which ones are the best to travel with. They can ask about their environmental policies, their contribution to the communities they operate in, and their policy on training and employing local people.

A number of organizations offer such information for people interested in sustainable tourism. For example, in the USA The International Ecotourism Society (TIES) runs a website service called 'Your Travel Choice Makes A Difference' and the UK-based Tourism Concern has produced *The Good Alternative Travel Guide* to inform tourists about operators offering holidays that directly benefit local people.

Once at their destination, tourists can spread the benefits of their stay to local communities by

VIEWPOINTS

'Feedback is the best way to effect change. If their clientele don't care if they recycle, the hotels won't either'
Patricia Griffin, President, Green Hotels Association

'We can encourage our guests to be greener, but we can't dictate how they should respond'
Neil Jacobs, Group Director, Four Seasons Resort, Singapore

supporting cafés or craft shops rather than always buying their food and souvenirs at their hotel. Not only does this put money directly into local communities, but it can also provide interesting insights into the people and places visited.

Buying local food, as these tourists are in Bangkok, Thailand, ensures that local people benefit from tourist spending.

If tourists see something they feel is unsustainable, such as excessive waste, they should report it to the resort manager or tour operator. These companies want contented visitors, so if enough people complain about issues they are sure to make changes. We should all take our personal responsibility seriously – as tourists we have the power to make a difference!

DEBATE

Imagine you were in charge of inspecting a resort to see how sustainable it was. What criteria (or measures) would you use to carry out your inspection?

THE FUTURE OF TOURISM

From boom to the moon!

At the start of the twenty-first century tourism is one of the world's biggest industries and, if current trends continue, it is set to become even bigger. Technology is making new areas more accessible and allowing more and more people to find out about them through the media and the Internet. Even the moon is now within reach. In April 2001 an American businessman, Dennis Tito, became the world's first space tourist, paying US$20 million for a ticket to the International Space Station. He was followed in 2002 by Mark Shuttleworth from South Africa who paid a similar amount and sparked serious discussions about the possibility of space tourism. Although it may seem unlikely to most people, companies in Russia and the USA are taking the idea seriously and have already designed prototype tourist spaceships and orbiting stations.

This view of the Earth from space might one day be in many family albums if space tourism becomes a reality in the future.

Cure or curse?

Back on Earth, tourism continues to spread to previously remote places, with visitor numbers in some locations increasing at alarming rates. Much of this growth is taking place in less developed regions where tourism offers great promise of jobs and incomes. Governments, keen to cash in, have often opened up their countries to tourism with little thought as to the environmental and social consequences. Local communities have lost their land and faced competition for scarce resources such as water and timber. Cultures have been commercialized or in some cases virtually eliminated and economies have become over-dependent on tourist earnings that could vanish at any moment.

> **FACT**
>
> Between 1997 and 2000, Internet bookings of flights and other travel services increased by 500 per cent.

Turning the tide

Now people and organizations everywhere are realizing that tourism needs to be better regulated. Tourists themselves have been at the forefront of this realization and, thanks to a few leading examples, new forms of more responsible and sustainable tourism are rapidly emerging. As they gain popularity, however, there is a risk that they will be hijacked by existing tour companies and reduced to little more than a new 'brand name' for an old product. In addition, regulations and controls are at the moment largely voluntary and too varied and complex for the average tourist to make sense of.

Local people surround a tourist relaxing on a beach in Goa, India, trying to sell him souvenirs. Is this a positive or negative aspect of tourism?

VIEWPOINT

'Tourism in the 21st century will not only be the planet's biggest industry, it will be the largest by far that the world has ever seen.'
Francesco Frangialli, Secretary-General, World Tourism Organization

Why travel?

As more of us take to the skies in search of new experiences and destinations, some are urging us to think again about travelling and to look at tourism options closer to home. Not only are these often less polluting, they can also be less stressful, with less risk of delays, and greater familiarity with languages and money. Yet it is a reflection of the modern tourism industry, and particularly the success of cheap package tours, that many young people in the UK will be more familiar with distant beaches or cities than they are with their own country's coasts or historic towns. Rediscovering what our own countries have to offer could bring some welcome surprises as well as contributing towards a brighter tourism future.

Back to basics

Critics of the tourist industry are urging it to get back to its roots – when young eighteenth-century English aristocrats were sent off on a Grand Tour of Europe as part of their education, in order to learn about history, geography and the arts. Most modern

The Bedouin people of Egypt are very generous hosts to the relatively few tourists who take the time to get to know them.

tourism has left these educational principles well behind. Indeed, many tourists may not even engage with local people, see the local environment or taste the local food. However, there are examples which show that tourism can again be attached to these principles. We have seen that communities can benefit, that environments and wildlife can be preserved, and that local cultures can be respected and strengthened. The lessons learned from this growing number of positive examples now need to be transferred into policies and guidelines for the future. These should apply to the entire tourist industry – and mass tourism in particular.

These tourists are learning from a local guide about the uses of plants in northern Kenya. Education was the original purpose of tourism, something that is often forgotten today.

Take it personally!

It is up to each of us as individuals to turn holidays into experiences that benefit not only ourselves, but also those who host us on our travels. In doing so, we will gain greater awareness of the world around us and the impact we are having on it. We will also be able to share our experiences as we strive to create a fairer, more sustainable future – a future in which tourism is set to play a major role.

DEBATE

Having read this book, what would you advise friends or family members to think about before they booked their next holiday? Have your own views about travelling changed? If so, why?

GLOSSARY

adventure tourism tourism where the main activity is an adventurous outdoor pursuit such as bungee jumping, river rafting, mountain trekking or overland touring.

all-inclusive resort a self-contained, secure resort containing everything from accommodation, food and shops to childcare, entertainment and leisure facilities.

artefacts handmade objects, such as tools or ornaments, which have particular cultural interest.

backpackers tourists who choose to travel independently, organizing their own route. They often take their belongings in a rucksack and tend to camp, or stay in cheap hostels.

city break a short break, particularly popular in Europe, typically lasting three to four days. On a city break, tourists spend most of their time in or close to a city centre. Popular destinations include Amsterdam, Paris, London, Edinburgh, Dublin and New York.

developed countries the wealthier countries of the world, including those of Europe, North America, Japan and Australia and New Zealand. People living there are normally healthy, well educated and work in a wide variety of high-technology industries.

developing countries the poorer countries of the world, sometimes called the Third World and including much of Africa, Asia, Latin America and Oceania. People living there are often unhealthy, poorly educated and work in agriculture and lower-technology industries.

disposable income the portion of a person's income which is available for spending, after paying tax and living costs.

domestic tourism people choosing to go on holiday in the country they live in. Domestic tourism includes day trips to theme parks and attractions.

ecosystem the contents of an environment, including all the plants and animals that live there. This could be a garden pond, a forest or the whole of planet Earth.

eco tax a tax that is charged to take account of the environmental impact of a particular activity. Several destinations have introduced eco taxes to compensate for the damaging effects of tourism.

ecotourism tourism that is sensitive to its impact on environments and local populations and seeks to benefit (or not harm) them by being there.

elite a relatively small group of people who have greater wealth and power than the rest of the population.

emissions the release of waste products (normally gases and solid particles) into the natural environment. These include car exhaust and aeroplane fumes into the air and waste water and sewage into streams or the sea.

erosion a process whereby something becomes worn (eroded). For example, the removal of material (soil or rock) by the forces of nature (wind or rain) or people (deforestation, vehicle tracks, etc).

game wild animals, such as lions, tigers and elephants, that used to be hunted and shot.

global warming the gradual warming of the Earth's atmosphere as a result of greenhouse gases trapping heat. Human activity has increased the level of greenhouse gases, such as carbon dioxide and methane, in the atmosphere.

hurricane a tropical storm with very strong winds and heavy rains. Also called a cyclone or typhoon in some parts of the world.

indigenous people those people who are born in and originate from a particular region or country, such as the Inuit of Canada or the Aborigines of Australia.

International Hotels Environment Initiative (IHEI) an organization that works with hotels and their suppliers to encourage good social and environmental practices in the industry.

international tourism people travelling abroad for their holidays, often to far-distant destinations.

International Year of Ecotourism (IYE) an international focus on issues surrounding ecotourism in the year 2002. Managed by the United Nations (UN).

long-haul destinations very far-distant tourist locations reached by aeroplane.

malaria an infectious tropical disease carried by infected mosquitoes. Malaria is common in Africa and parts of Asia.

mangrove swamp evergreen trees and shrubs, with long, intertwined roots, which grow in dense 'swamps' along tropical coastlines.

nature tourism tourists visiting natural areas usually in order to view wildlife and endangered species in their natural environments.

package holiday a holiday, usually provided by tour operators, where some or all of the following are included in the price: flights, transfers, car hire, accommodation, food, insurance, excursions and entertainment.

responsible tourism any form of tourism that takes responsibility for its impact. Sustainable tourism and ecotourism are often seen as examples of responsible tourism.

scheduled airline an airline that has flights which depart at regular, set times. A chartered airline, in contrast, might be for a particular 'one-off' flight.

short-haul destinations tourist destinations which are a short flying distance away and can be reached relatively easily.

sustainable tourism managed tourism which provides economic and social benefits without disturbing local cultures, the environment or wildlife and natural habitats.

theme park tourism tourism based around a specific theme park attraction, such as the Disney resorts in the USA, France and Japan.

tour operators travel companies which co-ordinate and arrange holidays.

Tourism Concern a UK-based organization that campaigns for fair, ethical tourism around the world. It is particularly concerned with the impact of tourism on local cultures.

unregulated operating freely, without restrictive rules and laws.

World Tourism Organization (WTO) a global tourism organization consisting of 139 countries and 350 other companies and organizations. The WTO shares and develops new tourism policies and also monitors the growth and spread of world tourism.

BOOKS TO READ

Global Eye: Issue 17/Focus on Tourism
Worldaware and DFID
(Worldaware, Spring 2002)

Global Tourism Development
Anne Kenward and Jan Whittington
(Hodder & Stoughton, 1999)

Off the Beaten Track
Laura Stoddart
(Orion Books, 2004)

The Good Alternative Travel Guide
Mark Mann
(Tourism Concern/Earthscan, 2002)

Travel and Tourism
John Ward
(Longman, 1997)

USEFUL ADDRESSES

Tourism Concern
Stapleton House
277-281 Holloway Road
London N7 8HN
UK
Tel: 0207 133 3330

The International Ecotourism Society
1333 H St NW, Suite 300E
USA Washington, DC 20005
Tel: +1(202) 347-9203

Tourism Programme
WWF-UK
Panda House
Weyside Park
Godalming
Surrey GU7 1XR
UK
Tel: 01483 426 444
Worldaware

Echo House
SOS Children's, Villages
St. Andrew's House,
59 St Andrew's Street
Cambridge, CB2 3BZ
UK
Tel: 01223 365589

Worldwatch Institute
1776 Massachusetts Avenue
N.W. Washington DC
20036-1904
USA
Tel: 202 452 1999

INDEX

Numbers in **bold** refer to illustrations.